THE B.E.S.T.

MARRIAGE

G000243568

If you are looking forward to marriage, loving your marriage
or living to regret it: you deserve the B.E.S.T.

ANTHONY DELANEY

anthonydelaney.com

ivychurch.org

ISBN 978-0-9571414-3-8
e-ISBN 978-0-9571414-4-5

DESIGN:
Art Direction and Grapic Design: Dan Hasler
Cover Design: Jonathan Ogden

IMAGE CREDITS
The following images used are taken from www.flickr.com
and used under the (cc) 2.0 license.

We would like to thank the following:
BEANS OR BEST? - Phil & Pam
THREE STAGES - TheGiantVermin
BLESSING - mydogivana
ENCOURAGING - St Johns House
SHARING - swambo
TOUCHING - MissTurner
FINALLY - Opt1mus76

I am my beloved's and he is mine.

Song of Songs

Love: A temporary insanity
curable by marriage.

Ambrose Bierce

CONTENTS

A man went into his vicar's office:
"You've just got to help me...."

BEANS OR BEST?

A man walks up to an ATM for some cash, but is met by an unwelcome word familiar to many of us: OVERDRAWN! He checks the balance of the account and finds, to his horror, that the unarranged overdraft does not merely amount to pennies. Or pounds. But hundreds of pounds! He knows this is very serious! He has no means to put the necessary funds in the account, so he goes back home and makes a terse announcement:

"From now on, this family will live on beans and beans alone!" "Why?" groan his wife and kids. "Because we have no money! We have lots of beans in the cupboard anyway, and beans are… cheap!" The family open a tin or two and share them out. They do the same the next day. And the next….

Now imagine another character. This guy is a multi-billionaire. He loves this family and knows their situation (don't ask me how – it's just an illustration!). He comes along, and without them knowing it, puts a huge sum of money into their account. It doesn't just cover the overdraft – it replaces the negative sum with a string of zeros *in credit!*

But they don't recheck their account balance and simply continue to live on beans. (And lo, the house doth stink!)

If you've ever been in that kind of situation, you'll know the feeling of dread that keeps you going back to the 'hole in the wall' to check your balance. It's the same lack of confidence that stops you *actually doing anything* that will **really** address the problem, and keeps you 'living on beans.'

A man went into his vicar's office: "You've just got to help me." The minister said, "What's the problem, John?" "I have to get my marriage annulled!" The vicar said, "Now, you know I can't do that, John. Marriage is supposed to be forever and you've been married less than a year. Besides, don't you remember, you took her for better or for worse." John replied, "I know, but she's so much worse than I took her for!"

Pass the Beans

How many of us settle for 'beans' in our relational life, when it's possible to have so much more?

Nobody standing in front of friends and family for the biggest day of their life, expects that it would be anything less than the very **BEST** – or why sign up at all? So why is it that some marriages flourish whilst others fail?

I'm meeting regularly so many people who feel their marriage is ultimately both hugely disappointing and deeply unsatisfying. I don't want that to be the case for them. Or you, for that matter. That's why I wrote this little book. It's an easy read with some hard-hitting advice learned at the sharp end of life variously as a husband, dad, pastor and police officer.

I've sat with and counseled people with relational difficulties since my late teens when I had to pretend to be older and wiser as a 'copper' in order to resolve a domestic crisis. I've prepared hundreds of couples for marriage and led their services when they have come together in marriage. I've sat with them again when it all seems to be coming apart. They often say they know *something* is missing, but they can't quantify it. I've learned something from those many hard hours in tense rooms. For more than a decade now I've been teaching the four easy-to-recall principles in this book that help people take responsibility to invest in their relationship – giving them the **BEST** possible marriage.

I have taught these principles to hundreds of couples I have prepared for marriage before they walk down the aisle; used them as a basis for talks delivered at weddings and marriage blessings. I have delivered this teaching in seminar format and some have told me it has saved their marriages. Wow. Others have sadly said it came too late and they had already walked away. I don't want that for you.

I hope and pray that you'll find something amongst the four simple principles to apply to your situation – whether you're considering marriage (or remarriage), you're happily married, or struggling in your relationship right now. I'll remind you of some ancient wisdom, brought bang up-to-date for the 21st Century as I aim to help you reclaim and recover the best for you and your husband or wife.

At times I'll call on you to 'check the balance' as you read – and from there you can move from beans to the best, where you start living on what's actually available to you.

The Perfect Couple

And let's just be clear. I am not writing this as a man who has always had an idyllic marriage. I don't write this book from the position of never having had a row, a cry or a broken heart. Whenever I read soaring divorce statistics I always think, "There but for the grace of God, go I."

You see, when I married Zoë everyone said, "They look like the perfect couple!" But we soon learned that we were far from it. There is no such thing as the perfect couple because there is no such thing as the perfect person! Two imperfect people joining forces can be tricky! Zoë and I have had some tough times. We have had rows, disappointments and even needed to go to marriage counselling to get us through. But we have had some amazing times too! We love each other deeply and are committed to our marriage.

I've been married for over thirty years now to the same wonderful woman – but neither us are quite the same for it! Lessons have been learned and many are still to be learned. But the bottom line is that I've told Zoë, "If you ever walk out on me, I'm coming with you!"

I think the reality of a wedding day is better captured by a video than posed photos. A marriage is also made up of moving images rather than snapshots of good or bad moments. Don't give up on your marriage by only looking at the still photos of the past! Imagine instead that there are some new, exciting DVDs coming!

Marriage is a great institution
– but I'm not ready for an institution!
Mae West

THE
PROBLEM

Many people I speak with have become quite cynical about marriage and are choosing to stay single instead. Others are deciding to get divorced. A whole generation of young people have seen the marriages their parents have got, or had, and decided they don't want one – 'Thanks anyway.' Strangely, the people I meet who are most cynical about marriage are the *same* ones who get most excited when their sons and daughters announce *they* are getting married! They don't seem aware of the apparent contradiction.

What People Want

The fact is most of us still hope for enduring love. We want passionate love, erotic love and intimate love. We ache for friendship, encouragement, compassion – a place where we can love and be loved, know and be known, understand and be understood. Recently I watched a daytime TV programme where couples had been invited to talk about how living together was best for them. They talked about marriage as 'just a piece of paper,' until, in a surprise move, a boyfriend got down on one knee and proposed to his girlfriend who, in floods of tears, said, "I thought you'd never ask!"

In every study about the quality of life in which people are asked what they value most, marriage comes first. Relational quality matters ahead of job satisfaction, financial wellbeing and even other close friendships.

This isn't Barbara Cartland writing. I know marriage doesn't always work. There is no magic formula for relational remedy if a couple has decided on going in totally opposite directions. But, as the world spins faster and faster, people are realising that they need each other more, not less. There's a reason life insurance companies treat married people differently – on average you'll live a lot longer if you're married. (What do you mean, "It feels like it!"?)

In our often disconnected society, in our crowded, rushed cities, a great marriage can provide a place of refuge from the cut-throat, impersonal world we inhabit. Marriage can provide an oasis in the desert. Marriage can promote good memories from the past and connect us to a bright future. If we're blessed with children in our marriage, rearing the next generation can help us find purpose, identity and a deep sense of satisfaction.

> When two people are under the influence of the most violent, most insane, most delusive, and most transient of passions, they are required to swear that they will remain in that excited, abnormal, and exhausting condition continuously until death do them part.
>
> ~ George Bernard Shaw, Getting Married

What People Think

When I was at primary school, I remember a boy called John who announced he'd changed his surname from one to another. Nobody could understand how that could happen. He explained that it was because his parents had divorced and his mother was remarrying. The fact that I remember it so vividly indicates that in the late seventies this was pretty much unheard of.

In my lifetime, the place of marriage in the western world has undergone massive change. The transformation driven by changing expectations in the roles of men and women has led to a total revolution in how people view the concept of 'family life.' For the first time in centuries not only is marriage a choice with no societal expectation on it, but the decision to stay or remain married if things get hard is also a voluntary issue. If you don't like it, you really don't have to lump it – you can leave it. Everybody knows this, including the children. That's why at various stages all three of my children have had concerns about whether their Mummy and Daddy will stay married, because they see their friend's parents divorce all the time. In one of my daughter's classes, she was the *only* child who was still living with her original married parents.

There used to be only two ways out of marriage – abandonment or adultery. Now in these days of 'quickie divorces', all that needs happen is for one partner to say, "I want out," and it's a done (or rather an undone) deal.

In the Bible, God says, "I hate divorce,"[1] but let's notice that it does not say He hates divorcees! God hates divorce because he loves his children and sees so many people hurt and damaged by it. In 1960, a divorce took place every 20 minutes in the UK. Since 1980, a divorce has taken place every 3 minutes.

---

1 Malachi 2:16 (Malachi was an Old Testament prophet writing hundreds of years BC — divorce is of course not a new phenomenon!)

Around 107,000 people a year divorce in the UK, the divorce capital of Europe. 42% of marriages end in divorce, and half of those do so in the first ten years. I have seen a world of pain from those getting or going through divorces. There is an even higher rate of attrition amongst second marriages – which compounds and multiplies the suffering for everybody involved, especially children.[2]

What People Fear

So, whilst I am aware how awful a bad marriage can be, and that at times there is a need for divorce, I'm equally sure that it is sometimes a decision made too lightly. If you are reading this because you're considering that particular path, I urge you to tread slowly and carefully. Divorce may not lead to the rosy future it seems to promise. I believe for many people – maybe even potentially for you right now – there is a much better way.

The increased accessibility and the alarmingly high statistics of divorce go through the minds of many of the young men and women that I speak to these days. As I prepare couples for marriage, I am aware that at the back of their minds some of them have worries about whether their marriage will go the distance. Even as they walk down the aisle the bride or groom may have big questions and doubts because they know the odds are stacked against them.

---

2 One in five men and women divorcing in England and Wales in 2005 had a previous marriage ending in divorce. This proportion has been increasing each year and has nearly doubled since 1981, when 1 in 10 men and women divorcing had a previous marriage ending in divorce.

May the Force be With You

Think of marriage as an institution that is acted upon by centripetal forces (which pull inwards) and centrifugal forces (which pull outwards).

There once was a day when the centripetal forces, like 'what people will think', tradition, family, parental influence and the law were much greater at pushing people together in marriage than those forces acting to pull a marriage apart; even such things as infidelity, financial problems, unfulfilled expectations or the longing for a new deal. Now those centripetal forces have been stripped away so that the balance has changed. People are not strong enough to keep those forces at bay that would, unchecked, tear the union apart.

Houses That Fall

I often think that of all the stories one could tell at a wedding, perhaps the most well known but not normally applied in that context would be the tale of the Three Little Pigs! In the story, what really matters is what the pigs build the house from. The wolf comes to every house, doesn't he?

In the same way, the 'wolf' comes to every marriage. And not only does he come, but he comes with his big, bad, ugly, destructive breath.

He's experienced. He has blown down a LOT of houses.
He's hungry. He knows if he blows the house down, he gets a bigger dinner.
He's ruthless. He doesn't care who's inside.

He's persistent. Dwellings of sticks and straw aren't going to last. Not for long. He knows that.

So he huffs one way, then puffs the next. Different types of breath – the same intent. Then he watches and waits to see what will happen.

You know the story? When the first little pig built the house of straw the wolf came along and blew the house down instantly. You and I know some marriages like that – it's all over... quicker than you can say 'Love Island'.

The second little pig's a tad wiser. He makes a stronger house out of twigs. But that house can't withstand the 'huff and puff' either. We all know marriages like that too, don't we? They last a couple of years but then things go very wrong.

The third little pig sits safe inside his solid house of bricks. The wolf huffs and puffs but the house stays standing. When the wolf comes down the chimney, *he* ends up defeated, with a burnt backside – because he finds a fire burning away inside! This little pig is prepared. His house is strong on the outside, but also keeps danger at bay on the inside too.

Houses That Last

I don't know how much of the Bible you've read, but let me assure you it's not all ethereal and flowery, but rather incredibly practical. Jesus once said this:

> These words I speak to you are not incidental additions to your life, homeowner improvements to your standard of living. They are foundational words, words to build a life on. If you work these words into your life, you are like a smart carpenter who built his house on solid rock. Rain poured down, the river flooded, a tornado hit—but nothing moved that house. It was fixed to the rock.[3]

What are you building your life and your marriage on? Where do you go for advice? So many supposed 'relationship experts' and agony aunts have a trail of devastation and broken relationships as the result of their *supposed* life wisdom. Do they practice what they preach? No. But Jesus did. He was a carpenter and knew how to build strong. He knew how to build with the **BEST**. Wise people build on solid foundations, according to a plan. They continually assess, repair and keep on rebuilding. And they make sure the fire keeps burning, too.

The wolf comes early on when a couple "leave their father and mother and become one flesh." He comes as they have to redefine themselves no longer as individuals or children but as a married couple.

---

3 Matthew 7:24-25 (Message Version).

The wolf extends his claws at mid-life when they begin to look at each other and see muscles turn to middle-age spread. They see faults in each other: "The person I married didn't have nose hair!" (At least, I don't think she did!)

The wolf blows hard when the children come along, and when they fly the nest. As retirement approaches and a couple who have allowed the fire to die down wonder as their lives move into a different phase, "Now the kids have moved on, have we even got a life together?"

That's why it's so important to build strong walls. Strong walls that help build a safe place to express differences. Strong walls that can handle anger and deal with disappointment and conflict.

When couples choose to marry in church, one of the phrases we encourage them to say as part of their vows is that they will love each other, *"for better, for worse."* Why do we say that? Realism – because 'worse' happens! A marriage is not just supposed to last 'Till debts do us part!' Crises are inevitable:

- A letter through the door announcing the loss of a job
- A family member gets critically ill
- A parent needs looking after
- Retirement looms
- Children grow up and move away

Every one of these, and a thousand other minor and major changes – external or internal (whether just another stage in life or something that we could never have foreseen) – can tear down the walls of the marriage and rip apart whatever is inside.

In recent years floods have ravaged much of England, but the cry is always the same: "Why were so many unprepared?" We can be the same in our marriages. The floods will come.

Let me tell you friends, a good marriage needs work in order to keep that inward fire stoked and burning bright. A mutually pleasurable sexual relationship has to be kindled and cared for. The sound of laughter has to grace the walls, so that we get a sense of perspective on our troubles and break out of boredom. Romance, trust, mutual dependency, appreciation and falling in love over and over again are not sticks or straw. They are strong, solid stones.

That's what I want to build my marriage on. What about you?

You have saved the
BEST till now!

Gospel of John, Chapter 2:10

THREE
STAGES

Someone said there are three rings of marriage: the engagement ring, the wedding ring and the suffering!

As I have observed it, most marriages go through one or more of the following stages:

1. Ideal

The wedding bells still sound in their ears. He still occasionally finds bits of confetti in his underwear. They buy each other little presents every week (it used to be every day, but they're trying to be sensible with their money).

He opens his sandwich box and finds a note to 'Snugglybum' from 'Cutems' – no special reason, just to say she misses him. He rings her at work and they discuss anything, and everything… for ages. They talk about maybe having a baby one day, after they've travelled the world a little. Or should they get a puppy? Romance and fun is in the air. They laugh. They kiss.

Ooh, it's so exciting!

2. Ordeal

The cries of the kids are ringing in both their ears at 3am. He can't find any clean underwear again. That big stupid hound has left little presents all over the living room again and nobody wants to clean it up. "It was your idea to get a dog in the first place!"

He opens another final demand and stuffs it in a drawer out of the way so as not to worry her. She rings him at work, but he tells her he'll have to work late. She moans. He snaps at her, while he tries to think how to get out of travelling to see the 'out-laws' at the weekend.

They are both very bored. And very tired.

3. New deal

They're looking for the 'way out.' Maybe that old flame on Facebook who's just added themselves as a 'friend.' Maybe that new guy from work. It could be anyone who makes them feel good. It could be time for them to bite the bullet and be 'grown up' about it and have a 'trial separation.' Anything would be better than this? Right?

He throws himself deeper into being successful at work. He knows he fails her so miserably at home. So, longer hours. More responsibility. More stress.

She wishes he could be more like the man at the office who always seems to understand, pays her compliments and makes her laugh. She tells her best friends that all she needs is some affection. He wishes she didn't freeze him out when he wants sex. She wishes they could make love like they used to and that he'd talk lovingly before and after. But he just wants to talk dirty.

Sound familiar? There is another way to have a new deal. Even the greatest marriages have their problem days or weeks. But I want to encourage you that whatever stage you're at (or even if you're reading this in preparation for The Big Day and all the little days after) you can have not just a bearable marriage, but the **BEST** marriage!

If your marriage feels like an ordeal, I want to help you make a strong marriage that will prevail. I have learnt that there are attitudes and actions that take our marriages from exciting to exhausting and finally… to expired. But I also know it doesn't **have** to be that way.

Here's the alternative new deal:

You build a relationship so close that your family and friends would look at the two of you and say, 'They have the **BEST** marriage.' How? Well, it starts when you receive your partner as the gift God intended him or her to be, then you become the husband or wife he wants to empower you to be.

You are each other's best friend.
You spur each other on to greatness.
You share your lives and hearts openly.
You give and receive comfort and support so you never have to face a grim day alone.

One day if you were blessed with kids, they say, looking back, 'My Mum and Dad loved each other – they had the **BEST** marriage, the kind of marriage I want to have.' How fantastic would that be?

Room for improvement

At whatever time you put the TV on, there will be a programme on about how to improve your house. Paint it white. Get a new bathroom. Declutter. The airwaves are full of it. But everyone knows a real home is not just about what it looks like. It could appear to be beautiful but be 'just for show,' like an elaborate 'house set' on a high-budget film. A house is not a home.

Similarly, a marriage is not just two people thrown together. It's two people grown together. That takes time and effort and thought.

I believe that in every house, in every marriage, there's a room. The sign on the door says, "Room for improvement." God wants you and I to have the **BEST** marriage. However good your marriage is, there is room for more. Room for better. Room to make it the very **BEST** it can be!

Naturally, writing this book has helped me to reflect on my own marriage. As I look back, it's clear that the 'house' Zoë and I have built has had lots of storms and the occasional wolf at the door. A lot of growth and change has had to take place in order for us to grow together. But, do you know what? It's really rewarding to build a house with somebody else who loves you.

In fact, I think there's a better word for it – it's a blessing.

TIME TO **THINK**

Why not spend some time with your husband or wife now (especially if you have decided to read this book together) and answer some of the following questions:

What are you building your marriage on?

In what areas do you feel strong?

In what areas do you feel weak?

What is threatening to attack your relationship?

How can you work together to build the fires of your friendship and love strong again?

THREE STAGES

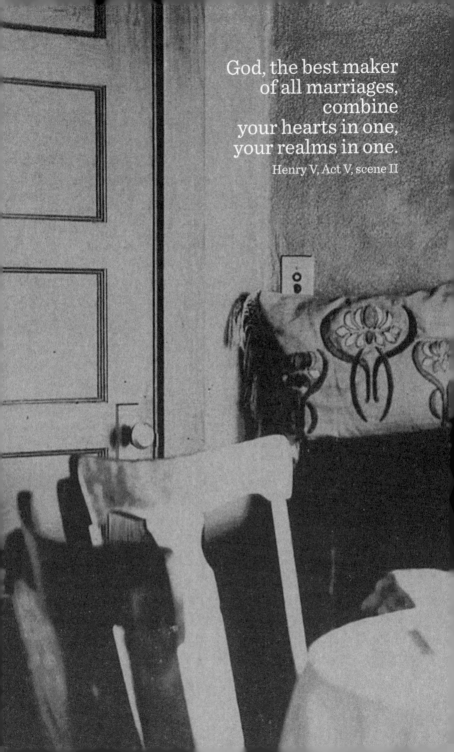

God, the best maker
of all marriages,
combine
your hearts in one,
your realms in one.

Henry V, Act V, scene II

B.
BLESSING

There's a trend these days toward having 'a marriage blessing.' Perhaps the couple were not married in church, but want the ambience of a place of worship and prayer to make it feel more lasting. Others want to please 'religious relatives' and friends. Some, however, really do want to acknowledge that they need God's help to build that strong home we've been talking about. Perhaps it's a celebration of a particular number of years together. For whatever reason, I think marriage blessings can do a lot to enhance a relationship. There's something very strengthening about a public commitment (or recommitment) to one another.

The power of the promise

When does marriage truly begin? It doesn't start with falling in love, because too often that is just about a feeling. It's not when people first "make love"; sex is a gift of God which blesses a marriage, it doesn't make a marriage. It's not when people first move in together and set up house, because there are no real commitments there. (In fact statistically those who live together before marriage are a lot less likely to remain together.) Marriage doesn't begin when a piece of paper is signed, that's the sign that it has already happened. So when does marriage begin? It begins when two people make a promise to be faithful until the end of their days. *Marriage begins with a vow.*

When the vow is spoken, something very powerful happens. Everything changes. A promise made, witnessed, heard, remembered, and trusted is the foundation of marriage. Not emotions. Not physical desires, personal needs or the practical fact of living together. No, not even love. A promise, a covenant, a vow. That's the spiritual heart of marriage, two becoming one. Dietrich Bonhoeffer was a great Christian leader who opposed Hitler. He wrote the following from a Nazi prison to be read at his sister's wedding:

> As high as God is above man, so high are the sanctity, the rights, and the promise of marriage above the sanctity, the rights, and the promise of love. It is not your love that sustains the marriage, but from now on, the marriage that sustains your love.... Free from all the anxiety that is characteristic of love, you can now say to each other with complete and confident assurance: We can never lose each other now; by the will of God we belong to each other till death.

I think that is a beautiful truth. Your love does not sustain and feed your marriage, but the other way round. The very fact that you said vows to one another supports your love. Those promises scaffold the passion.

In our marriage vows we stand before family and friends and make a public pledge, in the sight of God:

> ...To have and to hold from this day forward; for better, for worse, for richer, for poorer, in sickness and in health, to love and to cherish, till death us do part

The fact that these promises are public is so important. Did you know it's illegal to be married in a locked church? The idea is that anyone can walk in from the street, join in the service and hear these words being publicly proclaimed (I've led a few weddings where we have been joined by gentlemen of the road halfway through!).

So there's a public vow: to love, comfort, honour and keep each other. When we exchange rings we do it as a sign of our vow to honour the other person. Many take the ring shape to symbolise an unending eternal covenant. In the Christian marriage service these rings represent something wonderful as the couple promise:

> With my body I honour you, all that I am I give to you, and all that I have I share with you, within the love of God, Father, Son and Holy Spirit.

I don't know where you are right now in thinking about God on a personal level, but my belief and experience is that He has a plan for your life. I listen to people's stories of how they met and I think time and time again, "It's no accident that you met! There was a divinely appointed destiny happening!" Your marriage is part of God's purpose for your life. You didn't meet 'by chance.' I don't think anything can happen by chance anyway because chance is not a causative force.

And if you didn't meet by chance and marriage is God's plan, then maybe your marriage still has life left in it?

The beauty of the blessing

Three separate times in my wedding, the vicar said these words, which I believe have been prophetic. Since then, at almost every wedding I have officiated I have felt prompted to say the same thing to the wedding couple:

God has brought you two together, and it is His intention that you stay together.

It's important that you recognise that the person you married is a blessing from God. When did you last thank God for that blessing?

My friend Gerald Coates tells the story of Adam and Eve in the garden. He says that when God made Eve and showed her to Adam he said, "Wow! Why did you make her so beautiful?" God said, "Because I wanted you to like her." A few days later Adam was back with a complaint, "God, why did you make her so foolish?" "Because I wanted her to like you!"

The beauty of difference

When we read through the Biblical account of creation (right at the front of the Bible in the book of Genesis) we find that God made us different. Different from the animals. Different from each other. It's part of the plan.

We talk about similarities, but as I look at people who get married, most marry people who are their opposites in many ways. We are made different – and that's part of the blessing. It's a good thing. When you eat, you don't eat with two knives; you eat with a fork and a knife. Somebody said, "When two people always agree in marriage, one of them is not necessary!" You need to have some diversity. You won't agree on everything. And that is OK.

The fact is, while opposites may attract, later those differences can become an irritation when you have to live with them 24 hours a day. In marriage counselling I hear people sometimes say, "Before we were married we had so much in common, and now that we've been married a while, that seems to have evaporated."

If you're married, I can almost guarantee you that one of you is up with the lark and the other one wants to hibernate all day. One of you loves to talk. When you tell stories you have the 'gift of the gab.' The other one is really quiet. At a party, one of you is a social butterfly and the other wants to chat more deeply to one or two people. One of you loves to spend money. You're an extravagant spender. The other is (well) tight!

One of you is always on time. The other one is never on time. One of you is impulsive and daring and the other one is cautious and reserved. One of you is very decisive – you make decisions immediately. The other one looks at a menu for 15 minutes and still can't decide, then even wonders whether you should have come to this particular restaurant!

One of you loves to talk on the phone for hours, and the other is a man.

I am obviously painting a stereotypical marriage here, but you get my drift!

TIME TO **THINK**

Why not spend some time with your husband or wife now and answer some of the following questions:

What differences first attracted you to me?
How are those differences apparent in your marriage?
In what areas are they clearly seen?
How do you handle those differences?
Are they a source of tension and annoyance?
Do you think they are more obvious now than they were? Why?
Can you share a different approach and both be right?

The fact is your differences don't make you wrong – just different. Two people can express a different opinion or have a different habit – and neither be wrong. The most important question is:

Do you accept each other's differences?

Acceptance is essential to marriage because, as we all say, "Nobody's perfect." We all need lots of acceptance. Do you know the quickest way to bury a marriage? Lots of little digs. Without acceptance, you can nag your marriage to death.

Let me offer a personal example: One of the greatest ways my wife has blessed me is by lovingly confronting me about my anger. It didn't take her long to see that the way I dealt with frustration was by losing my temper. My background in the police brought a good deal of dysfunction into my marriage. Shouting and displays of bravado work well in the world of kicking down drug dealers' doors. But I have had to learn that they aren't quite so useful in your own home.

It has taken years of watching Zoë dealing with discord to help me see that there really is a better way to resolve differences of opinion! I didn't like what she had to say to me about my temper. I got cross at the very *suggestion* that I have a short fuse! I admit, to my shame that it's only in recent years that I have really received her message and started to act differently.

One day, I finally realised that she had my best interest at heart. (It took me so long because I'm thick.) Now I see that Zoë isn't looking down her nose at me or judging me. She simply loves me and wants me to be the best I can be; the man I promised to be when I married her; the man I promised myself (and her father) I'd try to be. She deserves better than a man who doesn't listen to what he needs to hear. That man makes her feel like she doesn't matter.

Trouble in the Garden

Going back to Adam and Eve, if you were to stop the average person in the street, "What was the first thing that was bad in the Bible?" most with pub quiz knowledge of the story would say, "It was the snake. That snake who got them to eat the forbidden fruit."

Wrong. Phone a friend. Or use a lifeline, or better still, read Genesis 2.

God said, "It's not good for the man to be alone."

Adam was in the perfect environment (the garden of Eden). He had the perfect boss (God). But it wasn't good that he was ALONE. The word for 'not good' could be translated as 'Not **BEST**!" Do you see where this is going?

God didn't just announce the problem – He made a solution for Adam! A special gift that was just right for him. He said, "I will make *a suitable companion.*"[4]

An opposite that helps

The two Hebrew words used in that ancient text can literally be translated, 'Helper' and 'Partly Opposite.' The old translations of the Bible use the word 'Helpmate.'

---

4 Genesis 2:18

TIME TO **THINK**

What sort of mates are you and your mate?

ROOMMATES: Sharing a home, but with separate lives

CELLMATES: Stuck in a rut, joyless but with no hope of escape (at least until the kids fly the nest and you might just break up then?)

CHECKMATES: A one-sided relationship, where one or the other has the upper hand and the other has to toe the line

STALEMATES: No one's losing, but no-one's winning because the relationship has grown so stale

HELPMATES: What the Bible says God made us to be for each other!

The reason the Bible ordains marriage as being between a man and a woman is precisely because of the way we are made – different. We need help from one who is similar enough to relate to us, yet different enough to not always agree with us! There is a divine purpose in the diversity as well as the similarity.

Unfortunately sometimes people have misinterpreted the Bible to attempt to control or subjugate but this is not about who's better or worse – the two don't compete, they complete each other.

It's always been true that God made us all with a deep, aching void for connection and relational intimacy. Lifelong marriage is one way that need is met for some of His kids. At least, it should be. We've all seen couples that are still together, but still alone. Maybe in our own families, or with friends we know. Or perhaps this is how you feel right now? You share a meal, but not a conversation. You share an address but not interests.

Let me propose an alternative – a wedding blessing.

Be a blessing!

You don't have to book a church to have a marriage that's a blessing. You simply have to *receive* the other person, with all their differences, with all the challenges of those differences, as being a blessing to you. Then – you decide to be a blessing. How?

We are a blessing to our partner when we discover what their needs are, and do something to meet them. Meeting your partner's needs can build strong walls around your relationship and fill it with trust, joy and happiness. Remember the illustration the book started with about an overdraft? You can make investments in your marriage just like someone would do at the bank.

In 1943 Abraham Maslow famously described the 'hierarchy of needs.' Most basic at the top of those are the physiological things necessary – purely for survival, the need for air, food, shelter, etc. Too many couples settle for just meeting those needs. They share a house, share the odd meal and give each other a lot of breathing space. Men think, "Well, I provide a roof over her head and food on the table. What more does she need?"

But that's not the **BEST**. Once those needs are met, we crave other needs that are just as powerful. All of us have the need to love and to be loved – to have life-long intimacy with another. We also need to be valued – more than this, even adored.

Marriage counsellor and writer, Willard F. Harley describes how inside each one of us there is a psychological 'Love Bank.' Emotional deposits get made in an account in your heart whenever someone touches a need we have and fills it. Someone pays you a compliment and opens an account in their name in your heart. You go to a date and start making deposits if you are attentive, polite, generous, and so on.

Obviously in a new romantic situation, both couples are initially firing on all cylinders to meet the needs of the other person. Singing, "I only have I eyes for you…" they will do whatever it takes to get the other person to be happy. Men are goal-driven creatures, which means even most men can be pretty good at this for a while! All too often though, after the wedding day, they put their feet up and reach for the remote, thinking – 'Mission Accomplished!'

> An object in possession seldom retains
> the same charm that it had in pursuit.
> ~Pliny the Younger, Letters

Picture this. A young woman working hard all day in the office meets a man who begins to notice her. His compliments make her feel special. He has time for her, makes her laugh. She feels like a VIP whenever he's around. He opens doors for her, expresses interest in her, and listens to her. She begins to open up more and more as she feels as though he's someone she can trust. He has been working alongside her on a project, and when she goes through a hard time, he's there for her. They finally meet the deadline together. He's grateful that she even bothers with him, while she finds herself increasingly drawn to him. She starts to imagine what life could be like with someone like him.

What's happening? He's meeting her emotional needs. He's clocking up deposits in her love bank a lot faster than the stock exchange these days. That's how many people end up with that head-swirling moment occurring where they say 'I've fallen in love.' The wedding day comes and the love bank registers 10 million credits!

But at the same time this pattern is all too common in affairs. When one partner or the other stops investing, someone else just might come along, meet the needs and end up causing a world of trouble. You know how the Bible puts it? *You reap what you sow.* What are you sowing right now?

How does a typical husband respond when his wife catches a cold?

In the first year of marriage:

He says, "Oh Sugar Dumpling! I'm really worried about my baby girl. You've got a bad sniffle, and there are so many terrible viruses going around these days! I'm taking you to the hospital, darling. I've reserved a private room for you. I know the food's not very nice, so I'll be bringing your meals in from your favourite restaurant. I've already made all the arrangements."

Second year of marriage:
"Listen, darling, I don't like the sound of that cough. I've called the doctor to rush right over. Now you go to bed like a good girl, I'll take care of everything."

Third year:
"Maybe you'd better lie down. Nothing like a little rest when you're feeling unwell! I'll bring you some chicken soup."

Fourth year:
"Now look, be sensible. After you've fed the kids, done the dishes, and mopped the floor, get some rest."

Fifth year:
"Why don't you take a couple of aspirin? I'm late for golf."

Sixth year:
"If you'd just gargle or something instead of sitting around barking like a seal all night...!"

Seventh year:
"For pity's sake, stop that sneezing! What are you trying to do, give me pneumonia?"

How to become a blessing

You can be a blessing when you put the other person first. The rest of the book really expands on this fundamental concept – but don't stop reading yet!

When you really listen to his or her dreams, doubts and dislikes – that's a blessing. When you enter their world – get to know and relate to their strengths and struggles – what a blessing! When you give praise in public and private – you're a blessing.

When you let the other person have room to wallow when they're down but you help them get back up again. When you come alongside and carry their burdens with sympathetic words and loving touch.

When you leave a loving note or call when you have to be away. When you say no to having to be away! When you initiate the hug, the kiss, or holding hands. When you surprise the other person because "you remembered!" and when they forgot or got it wrong, you said, "Don't worry about it."

The fact is we all have emotional needs. I believe God has designed married people to be the 'help-opposite' chiefly responsible for the provision of those needs.

TIME TO **THINK**

The top ten emotional needs common to everyone are listed as follows. Please note that they are not listed in any order. In fact as we will see, most of us will prioritise these different needs at various times and situations in our lives. What are the top three you really need to have met, as an individual? What do you think the other person most needs to receive to feel full of love?

If you get stuck, start with the one you definitely couldn't do without, e.g. when someone gives you their complete undivided attention it fills your heart up, but when someone peers at you over the top of the paper and grunts – you feel very low. You have a high need for attention. [5]

AFFECTION: Caring words, sensitive touch

RESPECT: Valuing your ideas and opinion

ACCEPTANCE: Loving me though I'm different

APPRECIATION: Gratitude for what I do

SUPPORT: Coming alongside and helping

APPROVAL: Affirming that you're proud of me, etc.

COMFORT: Empathy, hurting with me etc

ATTENTION: Enter my world, share ups and downs

ENCOURAGEMENT: Cheer me on, believe in me

SECURITY: Free of fear, I can depend on you

Now share with the other what your top three needs are. You will probably find they're very different or at least in a different order. You will never outgrow these needs. One of you might prefer to receive attention and the other affection. That's great! Unfortunately what sometimes happens is that we try to 'fix' the other person with what fixes ourselves. If my wife feels down for example, I would try to verbally affirm her and tell her how wonderful she is (because this works for me!) It won't do anything for her if all she wants was from me is to listen to her and give her a hug.

You will need them met every day of your life, and your husband or wife is the primary person here on the earth to deliver what you need most.

---

5 As listed by my friend Dr David Ferguson of *Intimate Life Ministries*

Blessing your 'opposite helper' happens every time you put your needs on one side, and choose to sow a seed in their heart. You count the cost of loving someone else in terms of your time or your money, and meet his or her need. You sow a seed when you seek the other person's fulfilment first. In my opinion it comes a lot more naturally to a woman than a man. So us guys need to work harder. Think of it like this: It happens when he hangs the picture that she's asked him to, before she has to ask again. It doesn't happen when she hangs the picture herself!

TIME TO **THINK**

It's the same one! I bet lots of you didn't actually bother last time I asked you – so now get serious. Read it again, and this time, actually do it. You are supposed to be the person who meets the other's primary needs.

How will you meet their needs if you don't know what they are?

Please. You owe it to each other. Go through the previous list of needs and pick the one that's the most important to you to receive. If you could only have <u>one</u> met – which one would it be? Write it down.

Having done that, try again.

And again.

You now have a list of your top three emotional needs. If someone connects with you and regularly meets each of these three needs in your life, look out – they're likely to invest in your love bank big time, so let me say this – **make sure it's the person you're married to!**

What type of thing would make the other person a blessing to you as they met your needs?

- Going shopping together
- A big hug or a back rub
- A surprise gift
- Going out to the pictures
- Being told 'I love you'
- Making love
- Having the dishes done
- A nice meal out
- A good talk
- Being told 'well done'
- A tidied room

You can be a blessing in lots of little ways. I don't know whether you're a person who prays very much? Surveys suggest a lot more people pray than you'd think.

I think you can be a blessing by praying for your spouse. Not just a general prayer, mentioning them by name and asking God to bless them (though that's a great start), but a prayer that reminds you how special they are to you, and thanking God for the blessing of your 'opposite helper.'

I'm praying now – "Lord, help me to rejoice in the love I share with Zoë and the joy and beauty she brings to my life. Bless her with your presence today. Guide her in all that she does. May she be a blessing to the patients as she works for you at the hospital today. Bring her safely home. And help me be a blessing to her when she returns. Help me to pay full attention to her and be humble enough to listen to her advice. Thank you God that she's not like me!"

I encourage you to write out a short prayer of blessing for the other person. I have to admit I don't pray that kind of prayer anything like often enough. But I do want to be a blessing for my wife, and verbalising that desire in prayer before God helps me to make it so. You may not believe in God. Well, if He's not there – what have you got to lose? And if He is, and He answers prayer – as I believe He really does – well, there is everything to gain! Plus the **BEST** is yet to come.

If you have become aware, as you have read this chapter, that someone else has been getting dangerously close to having a competing account, I implore you – close it down! Do whatever it takes to back out and away from that relationship. Remember…

The other man's grass may look greener, but it still needs mowing!

You can build the **B.E.S.T.** marriage – by being a **B.**lessing!

E.

ENCOURAGING

Nearly all marriages, even happy ones,
are mistakes: in the sense that almost
certainly (in a more perfect world,
or even with a little more care in this
very imperfect one) both partners might
be found more suitable mates.
But the real soul-mate is the one
you are actually married to.

J. R. R. Tolkien

The second thing to work on if you want the **BEST** marriage possible is encouraging your partner. I think encouraging is all about supporting one another. There's a word in the Bible that trips a lot of people up because it talks about **submission**. It says wives should submit to their husbands – and vice versa.

When I was a boy, I used to watch the wrestling on TV with improbably named wrestlers like 'Kendo Nagasaki' and 'Giant Haystacks.' The bout could be won by "Three falls, two submissions or a knock-out!" Hardly a good picture for marriage! But if you think about the word 'sub-mission' it literally breaks down into 'getting under' (sub) the mission of the other person. Getting behind them and cheering them on and helping them be all they can be. Sounds more like encouraging now doesn't it?

Another Biblical word we could have used is **edifying** – lifting someone up and supporting them. Ever seen a child sitting on a swing, unable to get it going? Just one or two little pushes and before long they're firing their legs backward and forward, able to keep going for ages. Some people simply need to give their partner the push! (In the best sense!)

It's so easy to say the negative thing isn't it? But you release power into your partner by being their number one cheerleader. In case you're fumbling around for the kind of thing to say, imagine how you'd feel if someone regularly took time to verbally encourage you like this:

I'm proud of you. I'm here for you. Brilliant!

Magnificent, I knew you could do it.

I'm praying for you.

You're very special to me.

I trust you.

Well done you!

You look so beautiful today.

You're so creative.

You make my day.

You're a joy.

You're such a good listener.

I love you.

That was the most fun I've ever had (with my clothes on!)

Thanks for remembering.

You're the greatest!

I couldn't be more proud of you.

You light up my day.

You're wonderful.

I'm right behind you.

Great idea!

Tremendous!

You're a great Dad/Mum.

You're God's best gift to me.

Terrific!

Good for you!

Of course the secret's in the timing.

The time to encourage is **NOW**.

I have kicked myself many times because I hung back with my compliments instead of taking the time to just come out and say it at the right time. Having said that, it's still better to say it, even if it feels too late! So don't be miserly with your praise. Encouragement can sometimes make someone's year!

The four-minute rule

Do you know what the most critical time of your day as a couple is? According to psychologists, there are two.[6] The first is the four minutes after you get up in the morning. Those minutes kick off the rest of the day. If you have things 'left over' from the day before, those first four minutes aren't going to be great. That's probably why the Bible says we should make sure we've got our forgiving done before the night sets in – '*Do not let the Sun go down while you are still angry.*'[7]

On June 1, 2006, Percy Arrowsmith (105 years old), and his wife Florence (100) celebrated their 80th wedding anniversary. According to the Guinness World Record authorities, the couple held the record for the longest marriage, and the oldest aggregate age of a married couple.

The two claimed the key to their long marriage was that verse I just mentioned about not letting '*the sun go down on your anger.*' They would not to go to sleep on an argument. They said they always kissed each other and held hands each night before going to bed.

---

6 From Leonard Zunin, in Contact: The First Four Minutes, quoted in Keep The Fire Glowing: How A Loving Marriage Builds A Loving Family, by Pat and Jill Williams (with Jerry Jenkins), Revell.
7 Ephesians 4:26

I think this is amazing advice. (Incidentally, if you live somewhere like Iceland where it's hardly ever sunny in the day, you have your work cut out on this one!)

Guess when the other crunch time is? The first four minutes you share together after you have been apart. If you have a regular day job, those few minutes when you come back together will set the tone for the rest of the evening. Not just for you, but for your children too.

Think about it for a minute. I know that John Gray (author of *Men are from Mars, Women are from Venus*) says that men need to go to their 'cave' and chill out a bit before they can face the transition from the world of work to the domestic setting. But there are ways to do that and ways not to do it. Rather than expecting or demanding my 'cave' time – why can't I submit in a loving way to what my wife needs? After all, I did promise when we got married that I'd do just that didn't I? Much of what passes as good relationship advice in some books can be misused as reasons to be downright selfish.

How do you feel when your partner walks in the house and starts grumbling and moaning about their day, especially if you've had a marvellous day and are in a great mood? I tend to resent that, especially if there are things I want to unload too. If we're not careful, glumness can spoil the whole evening. We should try to keep those eight minutes as positive as possible.

Can we take time to notice and say something when our partner has faced someone being rude to them at work, or to recognise and praise that they've handled a difficult situation really well?

TIME TO **THINK**

Why not make a conscious decision now that first thing tomorrow, you will be a source of encouragement – as soon as your head comes off the pillow. Then remember again to be that tone and mood setter as soon as you see your husband or wife after work. If we do this, then the stresses we are under won't seem half as bad, because we won't feel as though we are having to face them alone.

Contentment vs. resentment

Let me say something to the men. I was just in a bookshop and saw a book called 'What men know about women.' I opened the book – every page was blank!

That shouldn't be true of you and me. The word '*husband*' comes from two Latin words which mean 'house band.' Literally, husbands, we are to be the band that holds the family together. You can do a lot of that by encouraging your wife. So, when you are with your wife in a public setting, are you always correcting her? "No, it wasn't red, it was blue." You shouldn't do that. Make eye contact with her. Support her. Compliment her in front of others publicly and do it privately. Are you lifting her up with your words? Encouraging one another comes out of being content with each other.

On a scale of 1 to 10, how content are you with your partner?

Encouraging can bring positive change. But a spirit of dissatisfaction and trying to 'fix' the other person will only lead to resentment.

If you are bored with him
If you compare her negatively with other women
If you are usually negative
If you refuse to change yourself but always point the finger across the lounge at the person who really needs to change…

…then you won't experience blessing and happiness in your married life. You'll never have the **BEST**.

I have seen husbands and wives who have been married for more years than I have lived, one watching his TV downstairs, the other watching hers upstairs, living with dissatisfaction. Neither makes the first move or risks saying the word that would bring them back together for fear of rejection or a harsh rebuke.

People talk about 'getting hitched.' But it's so easy to end up living life on different tracks, only connecting at meal breaks and when the engines get put to bed at night. That's not the marriage anyone signs up for! We want the **BEST**.

More than a chat-up line

There is a Hebrew book of love poetry in the Bible called the Song of Solomon, or the Song of Songs. It literally means 'the best love song,' (though you might have another favourite). It tells the story of a courtship, a love, and a marriage. It's a description and a celebration of a husband's love for his wife and a wife's love for her husband. It is so graphic in its descriptions of sexual love that it had a rating on it so kids weren't allowed to read it.

If you took the time to read through it, you find it contains all the elements of every truly great love story. It starts out with the girl being shy and insecure. She's asking herself, "Why me? How can he love me like that? I'm plain, I'm ordinary." By the end, when she receives his love, when she knows how much she's loved – something's changed.

She stands tall.
She has been loved by this one who's royalty… and she's become a princess!

The ugly duckling is a swan! The love given and received changes everything!
Together, they're complete.

Throughout the centuries, Bible scholars have looked at this Song of Solomon and said that it goes beyond the realm of human love. Yes, it describes how a husband ferociously loves and cherishes his wife, but actually it is also a portrait of how God loves us. His love is passionate, fiery, extravagant and generous. It overlooks our faults and chooses to sees our beauty. It's the kind of love that transforms us from all we are intended to be.

If ever you read the Song of Solomon you might be surprised by some of the language used. There are many descriptions and similes that sound unfamiliar and even mildly unpleasant to our modern ears. Let me give some examples:

He says, *"You are the fairest of women… Your teeth are like a flock of sheep just up from the washing…"*

Now, that's not a chat up line I'd recommend. But in those days, she'd know he was saying, *"Your teeth are all perfect – they're white and small, in the right place and none of them are missing!"*

He says, *"Your hair is like a flock of goats…"* Don't try this one at home. I have no idea why that was once a good thing. Sorry! But it was obviously a nice thing to say back in the day.

What's he doing, this irresistible, wonderful lover? He's encouraging her. He's complimenting her. He is pointing out why he loves her.

And guess what? She's not afraid to go public in declaring her love for him, either. She says, *"How handsome you are. I love the way you smell. I want you to kiss me because your love is better than wine. She says, draw me away and I will run after you…!"*

She sees him coming toward her and she says (out loud), "He's like a gazelle – like a young stag!" No doubt that was the nicest thing anyone had said to him all day!

What a great picture of encouragement – building love that lasts. There's a fantastic vulnerability because these two people are so in love, they don't care who knows it. They tell it like it is. They say, "We don't care what the world thinks, we think the world of each other – so we're going to say what we love about each other…"

He looks at her and says, "You have ravished my heart…with one look of your eyes, with one link of your necklace… how wonderful is your love… your lips drip like honeycomb…"

Good stuff huh? The Bible is not just history or stories but contains wonderful poetic truth too. It is the Maker's Instructions for us – a manual for life now that makes sense of eternity. It can really help you and me in our relationships today.

How important is it to speak sincere, specific, personal and public words to lift up your marriage partner? Well, I believe it is vital. To say regular, genuine words of love to one another in a world that wants to tear down… nothing is more powerful! You are a blessing every time you decide that you will be the one who builds your husband up. You are a source of encouragement every time you compliment your wife at a dinner party. Or in the car when only she and the kids can hear.

Long ago, in Fiji, it was required that before they married, the young men had to bargain with the girl's father for her. The fathers of the village demanded payment for their daughters generally in the form of cows. Three cows could buy an above-average wife, and four or five cows a very beautiful wife!

Johnny, the brightest, strongest, and most handsome man in the village loved Sarita. Sarita was described as 'the plain one.' She was shy. She was also older than most girls at the time of marriage.

The villagers loved to gossip about the bargaining price of a girl. Some said Johnny might offer two or three cows. Others

TIME TO **THINK**

Take a moment and rate yourself on *speaking affirming words*. No one should either take marital success for granted or resign themselves to conflict and coldness. Instead, we should resolve to give our marriage at least the attention devoted to our car, by periodically refuelling it, giving it occasional tune-ups, and fixing what's broken. We surely owe this much to ourselves – and our children?

So give yourself a score – (low to high, 1 to 10), on how good you are at regularly speaking positive, personal, encouraging words to and about the other person.

If you are really brave, you could ask the other person to rate you too!

said Sarita's father might take one cow since nobody else w
interested in her. Johnny went to meet with Sarita's father a
offered eight cows for her.

Everyone was astonished. That was the highest price ever p
for a bride in their village! Soon, Johnny herded eight cows to
future father-in-law. The wedding was held the same eveni

Time passed, Sarita changed. Her eyes dazzled, and she mo
and spoke with striking grace and poise. People who came
the village and had never seen Sarita before remarked that
was the region's most beautiful woman.

Much later, someone asked Johnny why he paid such a high p
for her. Why offer eight cows when he could have had he
his wife for less? Did he make such an offer to make her hap

"Yes, I wanted her to be happy, but I wanted more than t
The most important thing that changes a person is how
thinks about herself. Sarita believed she was worth noth
Now she knows she is worth more than any other woman ir
village." Johnny concluded, "I loved Sarita and no other wor
And I wanted to marry her. I also wanted an eight-cow w

I have to say I can never understand it when I hear a husl
pulling his wife down in public. And I hear it far too ofter
they think anyone's impressed? Do they think it makes t
look clever? Actually they're saying, "Look how stupid /
marrying her!"

To keep your marriage brimming,
With love in the wedding cup,
Whenever you're wrong, admit it;
Whenever you're right, shut up.

Ogden Nash

S.
SHARING

I'm going to focus on one area that is vital in building a strong marriage. Sharing means talking. Talking about what matters. Being honest about what's really going on in your heart. Communication.

I married Miss Right.
I just didn't know her first
name was Always.
                    Anon

(Obviously Anon! Probably dead too...)

We don't talk anymore

Under the headline '*Married couples have nothing more to say to each other after 8 years,*' the Daily Mirror reported that the major dysfunction in failing marriages isn't usually sexual but verbal. A study by Professor Hans Jurgens asked 5000 German husbands and wives how often they talked to each other. After 2 years of marriage, most of them managed two or three minutes of chat over breakfast, more than 20 minutes over the evening meal and a few more minutes in bed. By the sixth year, for many that was down to 10 minutes a day. A state of 'almost total speechlessness' was reached by the eighth year of marriage.

When we were going out and in the first flush of love, I remember sitting in a pub together and looking across at a couple on the other side of the bar. They sat for hours and never exchanged a word. Zoë looked at me and said, "I wonder how long they've been married."

Now perhaps it's fair to say that some reporters make up German professors to sell papers on quiet news days, but it's also true that too many people just… stop… talking.

They don't plan for it, and they usually have stopped listening long before they stopped talking! They don't share their feelings any more.

One man said, "When I first got married my wife brought me my slippers and my dog barked. Now it's the other way round!"

A risk worth taking

I have to admit I like to watch shows like 'You've Been Framed!' Seeing all those crazy people having ridiculous accidents because they thought the partially-erected shed would hold their full weight… or that zip wire as thick as a piece of thread would carry them safely across the river… they really make me laugh! Recently I particularly enjoyed a show called 'When Stunts Go Wrong.' (You might now think there is something wrong with me, but I have a fascination to see daredevil types, jumping over flaming bridges or lines of trucks.) Even though the title of the show gives me a clue that this is not likely to be a happy ending for the daredevil, I find myself glued to the screen, willing them on – until the inevitable disaster fully unfolds.

I came off a mountain bike a few years back, suffered serious injury, and took a long time to recover. The experience gave me great admiration for the risks such people take, without ever wanting to emulate them!

But there's a greater risk I encourage you to take – in your marriage. It is the risk to be totally honest with your husband or wife. To share your heart. To share yourself. This is all about vulnerability. Something we can all struggle with. The Bible often uses the word 'intimacy' which could also be translated as *revealing* or *disclosing*. Why is it such a risk? Because humanity's oldest problem is the fear of rejection.

Most people go to the grave without ever knowing the joy of a relationship of total honesty. For most people, it's just too risky. Because we think, *"What if they don't like who I really am? Because, after all, who I am is all I've got!"* We don't like that. We'd rather jump the Grand Canyon in a white leather jacket. With fringes.

We can hide our needs or desires, while expecting the other person to be a mind reader. Harbouring resentment or getting upset we think they *should* know somehow – saying "If he cared enough about me, he'd guess!"

But when we hide our hearts rather than share them, we miss out on the **BEST** and inevitably end up hurt or disappointed. It's a vicious circle. Turning inward we seek to protect ourselves rather than share our fears, excitement or concerns. We don't talk about our money trouble or our time pressures. Instead we withdraw into the TV or computer, we over-spend, lose sleep, gain weight and become irritable.

Have you ever found yourself defending a stupid decision? Here's how it works for me. Fear of being rejected makes me get defensive. I *hate* to admit it when I made a mistake. I hate to admit weaknesses. I get it wrong, then make mistakes and deny them. Before we got married, Zoë had an idealised view of what I was really like – it's the only reason I can think she said yes! Before very long, the ideal me gave way to the real me.

Remember that stuff about Adam and Eve? Well you don't have to read very far into their story to discover what it looks like when we try to hide our true selves, and the consequences of such self-deception.

Whenever I look at this passage in the Bible, I'm always reminded of the story of the pastor who was going to speak on it. He stepped into the pulpit but was unaware that he'd dropped one of the pieces of paper he was going to preach from and it fell on the ground.

> He stood and started reading the scripture, "And Adam said to Eve.." He flipped a page and it was obviously out of order. "And Adam said to Eve... ...now that's very interesting, it looks like a leaf is missing!"

Adam and Eve ended up hiding in the garden, and God shows up looking for them. He asks them questions. (When an Omnipotent Being asks questions it's not because He needs to know the answers, it's because He wants *you* to!) Adam and Eve have a choice. They could be honest and vulnerable and tell the truth. But they don't. Since the dawn of time there have been two common reactions whenever we are asked to account for ourselves: Accusing and Excusing.

Accusing – If I tell the truth, the whole truth and nothing but the truth, it might end up with *me* in the dock! So if in doubt, blame someone else! I have faults, but I don't want to admit it, so I accuse the other person. The buck stops – over there!

"What problem? It's your problem. I haven't got a problem!" It's your fault. When God asked what happened – Adam took it like a man – by blaming his wife! He even blamed God for making her! "The woman YOU put here with me gave me the fruit and I ate it."

God looked at Eve. Would she be honest enough to share the truth? She replied, "The snake tricked me into eating." Ever since that time, men have been pointing the finger at women, and women have been calling men snakes!

Excusing – I excuse myself. I pretend nothing is wrong. If I ignore it for long enough maybe it will go away. "I don't have any problems in my marriage. It's fine." "I like a drink, but I have it under control." "Okay, my debts are piling up, but I can get another credit card – if the banks trust me, why don't you?"

But we know deep down that pretending doesn't work.[8]

What are you pretending not to know in your relational life? Is there a problem in your marriage you're pretending doesn't exist? I secretly smoked for years. I'd take the dog for a walk (the laziest dog ever – it hated walking) and have a secret cigar.

---

[8] The apostle John hit it on the head when he wrote, 'If we say we have no sin, we deceive ourselves and the truth is not in us.' I John 1:8

I was kidding myself that nobody in the family knew. One day, they all confronted me at once. My son's tears and pleas, saying, "Dad, we don't want you to die!" finally gave me the 'truth shock' I needed. I couldn't cover or keep that destructive habit – the truth set me free.

TIME TO **THINK**

I'm so glad they loved me enough to dare to challenge me. Now I dare you to stop the cover-up, and quit pretending. Is there an elephant in the room? Everybody's saying, "What elephant? I don't see any elephant." We walk around it, try to hide it under the carpet. Give the elephant a name and kick it out.

What are you pretending not to know in your marriage? What don't you want to talk about? What subject has you changing the subject? You know it's not going to get any better until you throw away the fig leaves. Drop the masks. Deal with it.

I have to face my faults if I'm ever going to be freed from them. The second wisest man who ever lived said, "Whoever conceals his faults will never prosper, but whoever admits and renounces them finds mercy."[9] It's not wise to pretend I'm perfect, that my faults don't exist. Everyone who knows me well knows most of them anyway!

Sharing starts when I don't condone my wrong actions, justify them or make excuses about them. Sharing comes when I say it DOES matter.

What are you defensive about? (Who? Me?)

The tragedy is that a lot of marriages have problems that can be solved relatively quickly *when you talk about them*. But we can be afraid to share the truth about ourselves and if necessary to ask for help. So the pain gets worse… and worse… and worse.

Remember these 4 'P's:
Pretending perpetuates problems – permanently!

There's nothing more wonderful than having a partner who's your best friend; someone you can just talk with, about anything. But the number one complaint I hear from women is, "*I don't really know what he thinks or feels about anything that really matters. Before we got married, he talked all the time. Now he grunts – and he only grunts when he wants food, sex or to change channels!*"

---

9 The Book of Proverbs 28:13

The alternative? Have the **BEST** marriage. **SHARE**. Start small if you have to. But be courageous enough to start to talk about your faults, your failures, your fears and (yes) even your feelings!

A one hundred year old man was celebrating eighty years of marriage. He was asked, "Didn't you ever consider divorce?" He replied, "Divorce? Never! Murder... many times!"

Tell the truth to each other. Care enough to reveal yourself.

Revealing your feelings is the beginning of healing!

I am talking about the greatest risk you will ever take in your marriage – I know it's scary. Not many people ever get there. But it's also the only way marriage can be the rewarding relationship it was designed to be. Intimacy only comes when you are bold enough to share. Share your faults. Share your feelings. Share your fears. The real you. There is no other way to develop real intimacy. That's the way to have the **BEST** marriage.

TIME TO **THINK**

When did you last share ideas? Dreams?

When did you last ask for help?

Answer silly questions?

Let your partner know how you feel?

Tell them what's bothering you?

When did you last give your partner your complete, undivided attention?

I've found this doesn't 'just happen' in busy lives like ours. It's important to schedule and fiercely guard regular time to talk when you're both in a good mood and can give each other total attention or the busyness of life will push it out.

> The great question... which I have not been able to answer... is, What... does a woman want?
>
> Freud

Listen with your eyes, please.

It's very important to remember that there are two sides to any communication. The best form of communication is made up of two good listeners. That's why when God put us our heads together he stuck two ears on and only one mouth. Listening to your spouse is important. How? Be like those people who take your order at the 'Drive Thru' – repeat some things back to confirm you heard right.

Arguments occur because we mistranslate what we think the other person is getting at, instead of listening so that we understand. St Francis of Assisi's advice was more recently repeated for our century by Stephen Covey who wrote, 'The Seven Habits of Highly Effective People.' He reminds us of importance of listening when he says we must *'Seek first to understand,'* rather than seek first to be understood.

It's easy to miss each other in our communication. In the church world there's a technical term used when one person is talking but nobody's really listening. We call it a sermon!

A golden anniversary party was thrown for an elderly couple. The husband was moved by the occasion and wanted to tell his wife just how much he loved her. His wife was very hard of hearing, and often misunderstood what he said. With all the family members and friends gathered around, he toasted her: "To my dearest wife, after 50 years I've found you tried and true!"

Everyone smiled approval, but his wife said, "Whaaaat?"

He repeated more loudly, "AFTER FIFTY YEARS I'VE FOUND YOU TRIED AND TRUE!"

She shot back venomously, "Listen buster, after fifty years I'm tired of you, too!"

A good mnemonic

That was the rules about listening. Here's a good one for talking. Alan Redpath said he always tried to remember to **THINK** before he talked. That's good advice. Especially when you consider what he said made up the letters of that word.

Ask yourself – is what I'm going to say...
True
Helpful
Inspiring
Necessary
Kind

With that filter in mind, we can start to share much more freely. We can redirect our paths, resolve unhealed hurts and refocus on what matters most. M Scott Peck, who wrote '*The Road Less Travelled*,' says, "*The road to intimacy is through the tunnel of chaos.*"

Jesus Christ said, "If you know the truth, the truth will set you free."

I hear you saying, "Oh yeah – the truth will set you free, but first it might make you miserable!" We don't like to face the truth about ourselves. We want to cover up our fears, our faults, our feelings – but that only makes things worse. I won't kid you that it is risky and can be painful, but the pain is worth the payoff. When you come through the 'tunnel of chaos' it means you stop communicating superficially about other people, events and so on. It is a necessary stopping off point on the road to intimacy.

TIME TO **THINK**

Hang on in there! If you want your marriage set free to be the new relationship your pray and dream about, you must share the truth and face the facts. Decide together what you want to accomplish. Tell your partner how much you value them, how appreciative you are of what they're trying to do to make your marriage even better. Share your hopes, dreams and disappointments. Thank them for being willing to talk about the stuff that really matters.

T.
TOUCHING

My wife is a sex object.
Every time I ask for sex, she objects.

Les Dawson

As a seven-time Tour de France winner, Lance Armstrong knew more than most about the importance of hard work. But in his book, *Every Second Counts*, he described his regret that he did not put the effort into his marriage that he did into his bike racing:

> All I knew was that in trying to do everything, we'd forgotten to do the most important thing. We forgot to be married. People warn you that marriage is hard work, but you don't listen. You talk about the pretty bridesmaids' dresses, but you don't talk about what happens next; about how difficult it will be to stay or to rebuild. What nobody tells you is that there will be more than just some hard days. There will be some hard weeks and perhaps even some hard years.

Comfortable affection

The final principle I want you to think about to have the **BEST** marriage is **TOUCH**. There really is no substitute for the simple touch of a loving hand or an arm around the shoulder. How great is it when a child you love spontaneously 'bear-hugs' you and then covers you kisses? Or when you feel a colleague pat you on the back and say, "Well done mate!" For some of us, that kind of thing makes us feel great.

However, others who haven't grown up with much in the way of safe and normal affection can feel uncomfortable when it is shown. They might say "Mum and Dad weren't really the hugging type, but I knew they loved me anyway." Such people can feel awkward when someone offers a handshake or a hug and want to retreat. Perhaps they think that affection is an optional part of living. Others still can *want* to be affectionate, but aren't sure how.

Necessary affection

No more convincing evidence of the absence of parental affection exists than that compiled by Rene Spitz. In a South American orphanage, Spitz observed and recorded what happened to 97 children who were deprived of emotional and physical contact with others. Because of a lack of funds, there were not enough staff to adequately care for these children, ages 3 months to 3 years old.

Nurses changed nappies and fed and bathed the children. But there was little time to hold, cuddle, and talk to them as a mother would. After three months many of them showed signs of abnormality. Besides a loss of appetite and being unable to sleep well, many of the children lay with a vacant expression in their eyes. After five months, serious deterioration set in. They lay whimpering, with troubled and twisted faces. Often, when a doctor or nurse would pick up an infant, it would scream in terror. Twenty-seven, almost one third, of the children died in the first year – not from lack of food or health care. They died of a lack of touch and emotional nurture. Because of this, seven more died the second year. Only twenty-one of the 97 survived, most suffering serious psychological damage.[10]

---

10 Charles Sell, Unfinished Business, Multnomah, 1989, p. 39.

If you had a background where you were not physically cared for, nurtured and cuddled by loving parents as much as you could have been, all is not lost! There is still hope for you. YOU can break the cycle and YOU can be free to express your emotions and affections.

Do you really want the **BEST** marriage? If so you may need to admit that the person you are married is likely to want your affection as evidence of your love for them. Ask yourself this: Might those closest to me have to guess or work hard to convince themselves that I care for them?

Many people in marriages are *dying* to be held – up close and personal. To be greeted with a kiss and a hug. I'm not just talking about sex here (unusually for a man!). I want to encourage you to make a regular thing of taking a walk holding hands. Take turns giving back rubs, etc. There's something very powerful about holding, hugging and kissing your spouse, not just a peck on the cheek.

Do what you wanted to be able to do when you first met but didn't dare to. Give them a great big smacker!

Health-giving affection

Did you know that there is scientific evidence that kissing is beneficial to your health? Psychologists, doctors and insurance companies cooperated on a research project. They found that the key to longer, happier, healthier and wealthier lives was the morning good-bye kiss. Husbands who kiss their wives every morning before leaving for work usually live five years longer than those who do not. A kissing husband has fewer car accidents, loses up to 50% less time from work because of illness and earns 20-30% more than a non-kissing husband.

One of the doctors involved explains, "A husband who kisses his wife every morning begins the day with a positive attitude. These unaffectionate fellows start the day with feelings and doubts about their own worth. You see, a kiss is a kind of seal of approval." There was an editor's note at the end of the article which stated that while the study only dealt with men, they were certain that it was just as true for women as was for men.

A man marries to have a home, but also because he doesn't want to be bothered with sex and all that sort of thing.

~W. Somerset Maugham

How to have great sex

Sexual unity is how two people become one flesh. It's the act of 'cleaving' to someone, whereby two separate personalities become a single unit. It's a bond between husband and wife.

I've sometimes had couples come to me asking about how they can reaffirm their marriage vows. I've arranged a public ceremony, when perhaps what was needed was a very, very private one, with only two attendees.

Five times in the Bible it says, "They were of one flesh... you will become one flesh." Sex, the way God intended, is a communication tool beyond words – a physical expression of a spiritual and emotional reality. The intimacy of sex makes it such a precious gift that it should be reserved for one special person.

Marital sex is shared vulnerability

The last chapter spoke of intimacy – and it's in the act of sexual union that we reveal ourselves to one another in total vulnerability. Souls and spirits connect as the body connects. Our culture encourages people to have sex to see whether the relationship might be 'a goer.' If they hit it off, perhaps they see each other again and start a friendship. But that's completely back to front! Sex is meant to be about cementing a commitment already made, a love already expressed emotionally, verbally and mentally. The commitment of the body is meant to come last. For good reason!

Marital sex is meant to be enjoyed

The Bible says that, if you're married, God's heart is that you enjoy your married partner. It says to the husband, *"Be happy and rejoice in your wife. Let her breasts satisfy you at all times. Let her love alone fill you with delight."*[11] That word *delight* is one of the strongest words in Hebrew. Other translations render it: *"be ravished, intoxicated, consumed, captivated by her love."* Not very prudish is it? In fact the Bible is very explicit about sex, because God delights in His children enjoying a sexual relationship that is mutual, exhilarating and fun. He wants us to have the **BEST**!

---

[11] Proverbs 5:18

There was a time when sex was known as *'the marriage act,'* that sealed the promises and covenants made on the wedding day. Without it, a marriage can still be annulled because it has not been 'consummated.' Every time we make love to our partner in a way that seeks to meet *their* need for intimacy and affection first; every time we celebrate each other's body in this ultimate act of self-giving and self-disclosure, we become one flesh together. We're back to the Garden of Eden – naked and unashamed, with no secrets. That's why God delights in it. It reminds Him of the way things should be.

The best sex is total, beautiful unity. It can make the marital grass so green that all the other grass looks brown. Every time a married couple makes love, they reaffirm all the promises they made on their wedding day and strengthen the vows and the bond of love between them.

Marital sex is good for you

Sex with your husband or wife is also good for your health. Regular sex within marriage actually reduces the risk of a man having a heart attack! Sex is such good exercise that you can cut your risk of heart disease or a stroke in half by making love to your wife three times a week. Interestingly though, having sex with a mistress has the *opposite* effect – the stress of infidelity *increases* a man's risk of heart problems.[12]

---

12 More Sex Please – We're Married. Andy Economides. Pg 52.

Marital sex is satisfying

My friend Mike Starkey wrote about this in his book, *God, Sex & Generation X*. While disturbed by our culture's obsession with what he calls 'Fast Food Sex,' Mike says, "Interestingly, surveys reveal that the people in Western cultures who have the most active sex lives, and with the highest rate of regular orgasms, are conservative Christians."[13] It seems true sexuality and deep spirituality goes together! The most sexually fulfilled women in the survey were the most spiritual women. Why?

Most books on sexual technique forget that the primary sex organ is actually the **brain.** The act of becoming one flesh involves a union of two minds, emotions and wills. This is a main reason the Bible forbids any sexual contact outside the covenant of marriage – because trust plays such an enormous part in good sex. If I just gratify my body but hold back my emotions, or switch off my mind, then the act can become exploitative and self-centred.

Marital sex needs to be anticipated

Remember those two magnificent lovers in Song of Solomon? She says to him, *"I am trembling; you have made me as eager for love!"*[14] What's the secret of being such a great lover? What did he do to make her trembling and eager? He set the atmosphere for love. Contemporary men are very bad at this.

We need to realise how important the context of lovemaking is, which is often more important to women than it is to men.

---

13 God Sex & Generation X. Mike Starkey. Pg.69
14 Song of Songs 6:12 (Good News Version)

A husband said to his wife, "I think it would be sexy if you'd moan a little when we make love."
A few minutes later, she said, "The ceiling needs painting!"

Women are usually much more aware of the context. This isn't just about buying a few scented candles. We men need to be more environmentally aware in the bedroom. And I'm not talking about using energy-saving lightbulbs. Some of what follows may apply, but you can ask your wife for a personalised list:

The door is not closed properly.

The curtains are open.

The room is too cold.

The light is too bright – or the light is too dark.

You need to shave/ shower – brush your teeth, gargle…

Take your socks off!

The kids are still up...

Turn the football off!

Affection is the atmosphere. Sex is the stratosphere! Throughout the day you can build moments of tenderness and kindness. Send a text. Call on the phone. It's the flowers, the hug, the listening, the kiss goodbye; the helping with the jobs around the house, all of this builds the atmosphere.

That atmosphere of affection can lead to the culmination of the event. But be warned…! Your wife may sense when your desires aren't putting HER first! Men – the Bible advises men to be considerate toward their wives. So think about her and what she needs from you.

Marital sex needs to be given proper time

A doctor friend who used to teach marriage preparation with me explained how men and women are wired differently. She said that when it comes to sex, men are like a light switch – they turn on and off very quickly. Women are more like an iron – they take time to warm up and cool down afterwards.

As I look through 'Song of Songs' I see how the two lovers prepared for their encounters and enjoyed them. They had special places for just the two of them. They dressed to be attractive to each other and guarded their privacy. They took their time, and had a lot of non-sexual affectionate touching. They used and enjoyed fragrances and perfume. This was not a 'wham bam thank you ma'am!' but a slow, deliberate, multisensory experience.

They shared their hearts (see previous chapter!) let each other know how precious they were to each other and how totally committed they were. She said (out loud), "I am my beloved's and he is mine," and that their love was "stronger than death." These statements show her commitment to him and her decision to stay within a loving relationship with him forever. There is nothing more important to know in marriage than the fact that your partner is deeply committed to staying by your side.

Forever.

Now that's what I'm talking about!

Let's Talk About Sex, Baby...

A husband and wife were sitting at the breakfast table, the husband reading the paper. The wife said, "Whatever happened to our sexual relations?"

The husband distractedly put his paper down and replied, "I don't know. Did we get a Christmas card from them?"

TIME TO **THINK**

Talk together about your sexual relationship. Be as open and frank as you can. Everybody in the world is talking about sex, except the ones who should be: married couples!

Discuss your frustrations and talk openly about your needs – what you like and what you don't like, what best helps you to enjoy making love and vice versa.

Be willing to learn, to experiment, to be helped by your partner to be a super lover! Take time for touching. It will create togetherness like nothing else can. It will encourage you to think less in terms of 'I' and more in terms of 'we.'

It will help you live in harmony with one another. An unexpected kiss, holding hands as you walk round the shops – the little affectionate things you did when you first met – do them again! There's enormous power in touch.

FINALLY

To get divorced because love has died, is like selling your car because it's run out of gas.

Diane Sollee

Suleyman Guresci, of Izmir, Turkey, divorced his wife of 21 years after a bitter six-year court battle. In an effort to find the ideal woman, Guresci turned to a computer dating service – the kind that evaluates your written profile and suggests matches for you. From a list of 2,000 prospective brides, the computer selected… his former wife, who, unbeknown to him, had signed up for the same service!

He decided to remarry his wife just nine months after their divorce, saying, "I did not know that my ex-wife had been the ideal counterpart for a marriage. I decided to give it another try."

I want to finish with a word to anyone who's really struggling in their relationship right now. If I could look you in the eye right now face to face, here's what I'd say:

Hang on to your marriage, and start doing the four things you need to do to have the **BEST** one.

As you have read through this book, maybe you've become aware of one or two areas in your relationship where you need to make a change. Don't focus for now on what the *other* person must do. What about you? How can you make changes towards being a better husband or wife?

Are you receiving your marriage as God's plan to bless you – and seeking to be a:

B.lessing to your partner?

E.ncouraging: are you cheering the other one on?

S.haring your heart: are you talking about what really matters?

T.ouch: do you need to reach out and touch?

Principles only work if you work them. But they do work!

A lady came to a lawyer and said, "I want to divorce my husband. I don't just want to divorce him; I want to hurt him badly because he's ignored me for so long."

The lawyer said, "You really want to hurt him? Okay – go back, and while I'm preparing the papers, compliment him every day. Tell him how great he is, what you appreciate about him. Build him up. Then, when I've got the papers finished, we'll serve them on him and you can drop him like a stone. It will devastate him because he will fall in love with you if you do all of these things."

She called back a month later and said, "Cancel the divorce. We've both fallen in love again."

I pray you'd have the **BEST** marriage, but for now – listen to this. I want you to hear that contrary to what you might think you may already have a 'Good Marriage.' There are probably many more positives than you can think of right now.

Don't listen to what the TV daytime chat shows tell you about marriage.

Don't believe what the glossy magazines advise.

Don't even seek solace in a divorced friend.

So many people have believed a lie that is breaking their hearts, breaking their homes and ultimately, breaking up the fabric of society:

And the lie is this: *'Your marriage is no good.'*

I've helped couples find hope again – even where there has been physical, mental and emotional abuse, or terrible betrayal of trust.

You have a good marriage because *Marriage is good*. It's a gift from God, and the Bible says He only gives one kind of gift: GOOD GIFTS.

Remember earlier I mentioned the phrase that was said three times at my wedding, "God has brought you two together, and it's His intention that you stay together"? Since the vicar said those words nearly twenty-five years ago, there have been times when it has been very important for us to remember them. I recall too that we looked in each other's eyes and promised that, with God's help and Him as our witness, we would:

Love, comfort, honour and protect – forsaking all others
Be together – *for better, for worse, for richer, for poorer, in sickness*
and in health, to love and to cherish till death us do part.
honour one another with our bodies, sharing everything.

Solemn vows indeed. As I look through the list there's times I've
not lived up to some of them. But I hold on to this: *'that which*
God has joined let no man divide' – which includes me. And you.

If you are reading this and you're already married, I believe
God wants you to remember that your marriage was His plan.
It was in his mind long before it began at the altar and it won't
end till the grave. In between there will be laughter and tears,
anger and joy, heartbreak and heartleap. But it was, and is, His
purpose for you.

God brought you together, It's His intention that you stay together – enjoying the **BEST**.

MORE... TIME TO **THINK**

1. Make a list of your faults, feelings and any fears you have about your marriage.

Prepare for a meeting and trust one another enough to talk together about these things. Don't pass the blame – fix the problems!

As you listen, look for ways to encourage and help. Remember you're on the same team. It may be painful to listen to some of the things your spouse needs to say to you. It may be painful for you to say some things you need to say to your spouse. But if things stay unresolved they can turn to resentment and cause terrible damage. **S**hare the truth.

2. Prioritise your relationship. Get a diary or calendar and schedule in regular times when you'll take a marriage MOT.

Ask:
Where are we going with our financial plans?

With regard to the children's future?

What are we going to do about holidays this year?
(Remember that a few short breaks are usually much better in terms of being less stressful than one major holiday)

What's good about our marriage now?

What's disappointing about it?

How are we going to meet the challenges in the next few months (what are they?)

What's our biggest problem at the moment?

How can we help each other? (Usually it's best if the guys just listen on this one rather than do our usual thing of firing off a quick answer!)

Be open. Communicate. Share with your spouse – so you can have the **B.E.S.T.** marriage possible.

Also by Anthony Delaney

Rough Diamonds

Work It Out